The Journey to Your Inner Freedom

The Ten Most Effective Secrets for a Self-Determined Life

REGINA REITINGER

Copyright © 2020 by Regina Reitinger.

All rights reserved. No part of this book may be reproduced or transmitted in any form or by any means, electronic or mechanical, including photocopying, recording, or by any information storage and retrieval system, without permission in writing from the copyright owner.

This book belongs to this traveller:

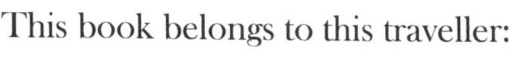

YOUR NAME

Dedication

Dear Reader, this book is dedicated to You.

Leave your everyday life behind and embark on a journey with me.

A journey into the inner realm of human existence.

As on every journey, there will certainly be different stages and even obstacles, but also a lot of new or known things to be rediscovered.

Let yourself be surprised and embrace the adventure.

I'm looking forward to experiencing this journey with you!

THE JOURNEY TO YOUR INNER FREEDOM

The Ten Most Effective Secrets for a Self-Determined Life

REGINA REITINGER

CONTENT

Foreword

Introduction

Chapter I - Who Are You Really?

Chapter II - Decisions

Chapter III - Needs vs. Selfishness

Chapter IV - Clarity and Action

Chapter V - Focus and Goals

Chapter VI - Agreements with Yourself

Chapter VII - Your Life – Good or Bad?

Chapter VIII - Mistakes – Opportunities for Experiences

Chapter XI - Be Good to Yourself

Chapter X - The Best Version of You

Foreword

"Investing in yourself is the best investment you will ever make. It will not only improve your life, it will improve the lives of all those around you."
– Robin Sharma

We live in a world of rapid change, and by default we are compelled to keep up, to stay on top. Survival of the fittest is natural, but in the process, we forget about our internal truth and identity. We move forward, often at the risk of losing our authentic nature and innate joy. The Journey to Your Inner Freedom is a step by step process to finding yourself, exploring your personal thoughts, and discovering the explosive power that lives within you. This is a power that does not kneel to fear. It is a power that attracts true universal connections, outstanding and natural achievement, and overwhelming peace.

If you are reading this, you have made the decision to awaken the greatness within you. This is a greatness that is birthed from truth. Your most pressing question may be how to keep all your balls in the air, while guiding yourself towards inner and outer freedom. By actively completing the exercises in the book at your own pace, you will reap the benefits of understanding your true nature. You will experience an impeccable revelation, where your effects on others is exposed and understood, and your ultimate capacity is brought to light. Self-deception will vanish and self-truth will flourish. The Journey to Your Inner Freedom is both subtle and explosive. It is both gentle and 'rip off the band aid'. It is designed to take you on an incredible journey, where you become the traveller.

Truth, freedom and achievement do not happen by accident. By discovering the best version of yourself, you can experience a life where everything is possible. In this book, Regina provides the blueprint necessary for self-transformation. She details the steps required to take charge of your life in the most honest and reflective way possible. And it is through this honest reflection that your higher purpose is discovered. In the time that we have spent together, Regina and I have connected over a shared belief that there is more to life than simply survival. We are both dedicated to unleashing human potential, talent and freedom, and this is one of the reasons I am so impassioned by her book. Regina combines the quest for a remarkable life with the pursuit of freedom and truth – a rare and powerful process towards soulful accomplishment.

As we develop through our lives, we are expected to understand, learn and develop abilities that are not taught to us. Qualitative decision making, confronting fear, taking action, and living in the moment are concepts that are crucial to a fulfilled life, but we are not given a handbook on how to implement them. The Journey to Your Inner Freedom is the handbook that you have been missing all this time. It is the guide to a fulfilled life through the expression of self, and the comfortable warmth that comes with self-healing and self-understanding. From this foundation, anything is possible.

Regina strips the mundane from everyday life. This journey of self-discovery is both unique and remarkable. Unique, because it is simply your own, and remarkable because it is an outstanding adventure that brings clarity and deep understanding. In reading The Journey to Your Inner Freedom, everyday life is left behind and a profound voyage into the inner realm of human existence follows. It is my deep wish for you, that by travelling your way through Regina's book, you will experience the value that comes with her secrets for a self-determined life. I believe that her approach is not only extraordinary, but that it encourages whatever it takes to find the real you. The you that is unstoppable, imaginative, powerful, loved, and above all, free.

Kane Minkus
Founder & President of Industry Rockstar® (Global Publishing & Portfolio Investment Company)

Introduction

This book would like to accompany you in understanding yourself and turning your existing life and ways of thinking upside down with simple tools to shed more light on them. When viewed in the light, some things reveal themselves to be quite different.

What we lack today in the Western world is not necessarily motivation. On the contrary, most of my clients, whom I have assisted as a business and life coach in the last few years, are very successful in pursuing their goals. What drives people are rather their questions of purpose, meaning, and true motivations. How do I orient my life? What values make sense to me? The questioning alone makes life along the lines of "keep on keeping on" no longer possible. If the accumulation of material wealth fails to give inner peace and contentment, then what?

Lack of clarity about oneself leads to lack of clarity in action and thus disorder in life. Although clutter may sap a lot of energy, it can be managed. A destructive, energy-sapping but somehow functioning life is not simply given up just because it makes one tired.

For evolutionary reasons alone, humans avoid the unknown and thus change. Change means leaving familiar paths without knowing what awaits. This means expending energy and strength towards an unknown result. And courage. The use of precious resources towards an unknown goal would have meant certain death in the past and it still feels that way today. Courage could help if not for this tormenting insecurity and the fear of making the wrong decision. In truth, change is thus a resource-consuming, dangerous endeavour that should be avoided at all costs.

Once you have been initiated into the ten secrets and have transformed their modes of action within yourself, you will no longer be able to confirm this sentence. For then change will mean the epitome of true inner freedom for you.

Repeat, skip, come back. Anything is permitted. This is your journey.

When I started to understand that freedom is not gained through fighting, but through understanding, forgiving, and letting go, I was already in my early thirties. That was one of the most important lessons I learned in my life. During the first stage of my journey, my life circumstances and my surroundings changed several times. Every change that took place internally resulted in external changes. I learned to see this as a natural process and stopped fighting it. I had installed my North Star, my meta-goal, without even knowing it.

Today, I have the privilege as a coach, trainer, and speaker to be able to reach people who want to change something to help them achieve their personal and/or career goals. It is deeply fulfilling for me to see what can be experienced and achieved on each journey. Cases in point may include a change in corporate culture that leads to a company successfully developing in a sustainable manner, or dissolving destructive personal patterns that positively changes a person's whole attitude towards life.

You might know the saying: "Follow your calling." Following has nothing to do with flight. One cannot run away from the responsibilities of one's life. And here often lies the difficulty. If you are dissatisfied with your current life, you first must understand the reasons for this, and what your own part is. Only recognizing and transforming these insights on the level of being will open the door to change on the action level.

I did not become a coach because it has become a fashionable profession or because I wanted to get out of the workaday world, but for the opposite reason. I went in. Into a fulfilled life of inner freedom and a profession that gives me the greatest joy.

Your calling can be anything. Every human being has their calling and their special place in life. Finding both is the individual task of each person. This might seem difficult at times, but those who seek will find. Definitely.

As far as my own journey is concerned, I feel that I have reached the end of the second stage. I eagerly await what the third stage holds for me. I will certainly have to meet some old challenges again, with others it feels as if I've moved closer to my inner freedom.

INTRODUCTION

To be free does not mean to roll down the mountain like a rock without a purpose and take along everything that crosses one's path. It means being able to stop to freely decide how and where to go next.

PATHS ARE MADE BY WALKING THEM.

– Franz Kafka –

It's time to start the journey.
Cordially yours,
Regina Reitinger

CHAPTER I

Who Are You Really?

> Man know thyself, and thou shalt know everything.
>
> *- Socrates -*

Who are you? A simple question that triggers a puzzled "Sorry?" for most people. What? Who should I be? I am Paul Meier, 47, married, father of two children and successful entrepreneur. I am an FC Bayern fan, my favorite car brand is ... A list of things we have learned about ourselves and that we identify ourselves with follows. Yet isn't that like describing only the facade of a house? But who lives inside this house? Who is this person without the ID card and football club, without the family and job? Who made the decisions, gained the experiences and insights?

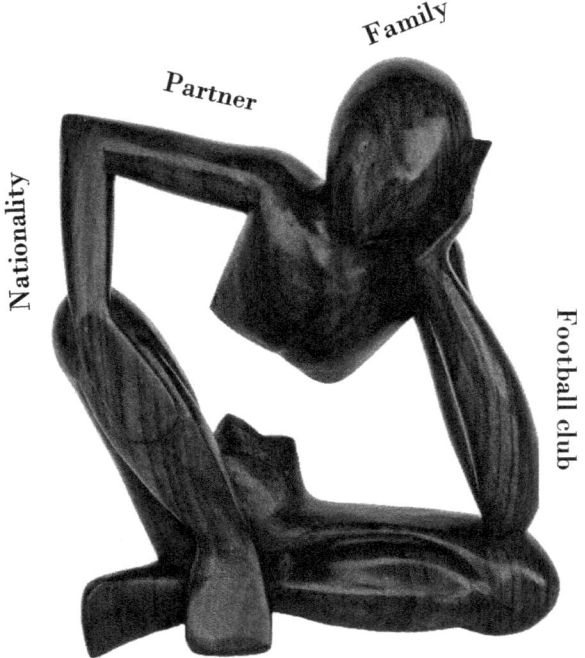

We are not human beings
having a spiritual experience,
but we are spiritual beings
having a human experience.

- Pierre Teilhard de Chardin -

What does your life say about you?

Take a short moment and look back. How did you get to the point where you are today? Don't think too much, just write down what comes to mind first regarding the respective decade.

Your life's timeline:

Age / Event

0 _____

7 _____

14 _____

21 _____

28 _____

35 _____

42 _____

49 _____

56 _____

63 _____

70 _____

77 _____

Reflective questions:

1. What do you notice when you look at your life in this abbreviated format?
   _____

2. Are there events that repeat themselves? Which ones?
   _____

3. Is there anything you would do differently today? Why?
   _____

4. Is there an experience that you would rather not have gained?
   _____

5. What would you have been spared?
   _____

6. What would you not have learned then?
   _____

7. Who or what is most important to you today?
   _____

8. Who or what inspires you in your life and why?
   _____

9. Who do you inspire? How / by what?
   _____

10. When do you feel really good / happy?
    _____

11. When did you last feel happy / in the flow? Doing what?

12. What has nature given you?

13. What do you like about yourself?

14. What do others like about you?

15. What have you learned from your mistakes about yourself, others, life?

16. In what respect / how do you think of yourself differently today than in the past?

17. Which difficulties have you overcome? What strength has developed through this?

18. What do you fear?

19. How do you want to be remembered by your family and friends?

20. What do you really want to achieve in the future?

21. From whom do you need permission to start your life?

_____

22. What decision(s) are you making now?

_____

Please take a moment to thank yourself for what is revealed to you and for having the strength to be honest with yourself. This honesty holds further constructive insights about your true being.

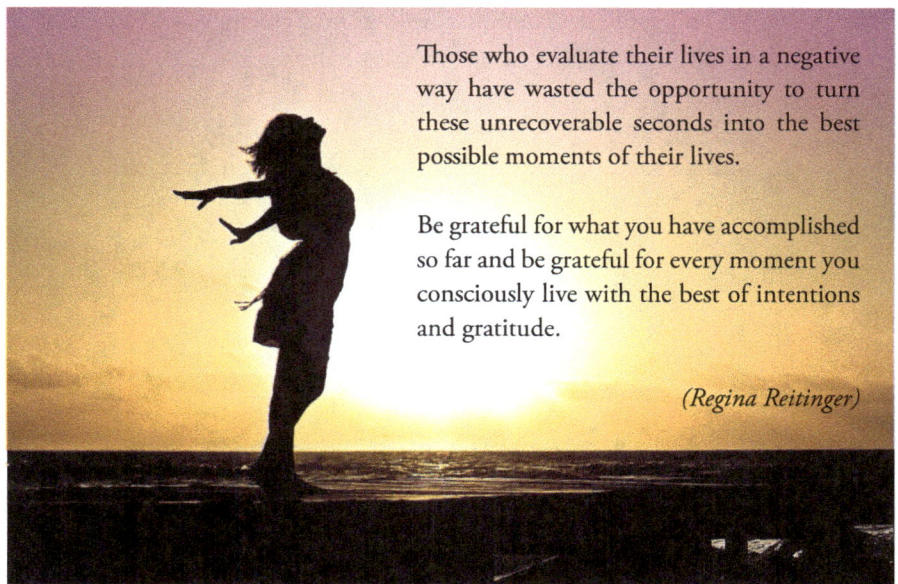

> Those who evaluate their lives in a negative way have wasted the opportunity to turn these unrecoverable seconds into the best possible moments of their lives.
>
> Be grateful for what you have accomplished so far and be grateful for every moment you consciously live with the best of intentions and gratitude.
>
> *(Regina Reitinger)*

Now please go back to the answers to questions 17, 18, 21 and 22 and write down the answers again right here:

18. _____ (Fear)   17. _____ (Strength)

21. _____ (Power)   22. _____ (Action)

Question 21: Who holds the power in your life?

If you are an adult and a name other than your own is written here, I would like to ask you to imagine the following:

On the day you were born, you were given a crown and your own kingdom right from birth. The purpose of that crown was to permanently remind you to hold your head upright and to watch over your kingdom. To take responsibility for it and to make sure that it is always well cared for and energetically clean. Those who take off the crown also hand over the responsibility for their kingdom and thus the power over their life to others.

Do you have the feeling that you are helpless, that you cannot change anything and that others determine your life, or that others are to blame for your misery? If you could measure that feeling, how strong would that feeling of helplessness be to you? The stronger it is, the deeper the scale extends into the minus range.

Power -10-------------------------------- 0 ------------------------------------ +10

Question 18: What is the name of your fear?

Are your fears general fears of the future, such as a fear of illness, poverty or death? Then please ask yourself what use these fears might actually be to you. In general, these fears make for nothing more than a bad mood.

If you describe fears that have more to do with failure / loss / or existential fears, then these definitely have what it takes to have a massively inhibiting effect beyond just causing a bad mood.

To be able to know and name one's fear is the first step towards getting to know oneself better. That may sound strange to you.

> *Why should I want to get to know this annoying fear?*
> *I'm happy when it's not there or when I don't see it!*

The strategy of giving fear a wide berth, of avoiding it or pushing it far away does not work, because fear works best when we do not (want to) see it. It often assails us in the most inopportune moments, so that we not only develop fear, but often even a fear of fear. The result: we distract ourselves, avoid the next step and leave the field clear for others. Simply put, others do what you dream about, while you stay far below your potential. The stronger the fears, the less your goals are likely to be achieved.

How strong is your fear? The stronger it is, the deeper the scale extends into the minus range.

FEAR -10 ---------------------------------- 0 ---------------------------------- +10

Question 17: Strength is ...

... expensive. What?! Yes, life comes at a cost! It will cost you a whole lot of illusions, to be precise. The first unhappy love, a bad grade, a project that fails, etc. Each time we pay a price, the price of illusion; and in return we get – reality. The currency for this is called experience. That's the plan. But we humans often do not keep it at that, we add an encore to the experience by evaluating it. The division into good and bad is something we learn early on and we thus deprive the whole of the deeper meaning of self-awareness.

Let's take the bad grade in math, for example. What does that grade say about me? Am I a lazy person? Am I stupid? Or am I a person who is (currently) not good at math (although I have studied for it)?

The difference lies in the way we look at things. While self-evaluation questions the whole identity and weakens the person, self-awareness focuses on the statement that describes a current state in the here and now. Such awareness does not damage the person in their identity. On the contrary, it grants the creativity of turning this so-called shortcoming into a virtue, so the person feels strengthened.

No matter what your experience was about and how much it may have hurt, the point is not to become scared, bitter or cynical, it's all about learning. It's about getting to know and understand yourself and grow as a result of it.

It is not the act of falling that determines whether we are strong or weak. It is whether we get back up and keep moving.

STRENGTH -10 ------------------------------ 0 ------------------------------ +10

Question 22: Which action do you decide to take?

One action can change your whole life – providing you act. Shortly before their deaths, a group of people were asked what they regret more at the end of their lives – the actions they took or the ones they did not take. The answer was almost always: they regretted the actions they did NOT take for reasons such as fear, shyness, or the misconception that they could do it at some later point.

Action is the only way to make dreams visible. Those who take action have conquered fear at that very moment and have won back a part of their kingdom wearing the crown on their head. Freedom. How strong is your urge to take immediate action on what you have decided to do?

ACTION -10 -------------------------------- 0 -------------------------------- +10

What's next?

What have you found out? Where do you feel things are lacking right now and where do you feel well positioned? If you have not come up with a clear and strong answer to this, you might have answered the questions in a superficial way. In this case I recommend that you spend some more time and take a closer look, to listen and feel inside yourself.

The frog jumps away from where it is too hot and kicks around wherever it gets too cold. It only moves little in lukewarm waters. It is tempting to delude oneself. But real change results from discomfort. Becoming aware is the beginning. Find out how you feel deep inside. Only then can you begin to understand WHO you really are and become the person you want to be. They who do not know where they're at also don't know where to start.

Who are you when you live the best version of yourself?

Would you like to take yourself on a journey where everything is possible? How do you experience yourself when you use the power in your life? What effect do you have on others when you consciously use your strength? What do you create when you act without being affected by your fears and do exactly what you want? Remember moments in your life where you felt that way – if not, please visualize such a moment.

Where are you?
___

What are you doing?
___

Who is with you?
___

How does it feel to be that person?
___

What is the strongest feeling you perceive at this moment?
___

What are the reasons for it?
___

This reflection helps one become aware of one's abilities. By remembering or visualizing specific situations, you bring your abilities and feelings into a concrete context, creating a powerful mental image. Your power image. You can experience the power of this image as often as you like.

    The more often you imagine your individual power image, the more you get used to this emotional state. Your body releases the corresponding happiness hormones and you not only put your mind but your whole body into the desired powerful state. From this feeling, you incidentally start to create your life according to YOUR ideas.

What is your higher purpose in life?

Of all the questions I ever asked myself in my life, the question of "Why am I here?" has been the most powerful one. What is the purpose of life between birth and death? Why are we equipped with all our skills and talents? So much power and competence only to give in to the oblivion of the daily madness that is exclusively focused on somehow keeping one's life running? There must be more to it than carrying out a job just to be able to finance the roof over one's head and other necessities. When you also consider that you cannot take all that stuff with you when you die, then that thought has a relieving aspect besides its obvious bizarreness.

The longer I thought about it, the more absurd it seemed to me that the apparent purpose of human life was to continue destroying this planet, generation by generation, while believing this could somehow bring happiness. No other living being would ever want to wilfully destroy its own habitat. It is said that man is currently the most advanced species on this earth. I wonder if that's why there is no real satisfaction despite days filled to the brim with work. Is our purpose in this life to wear ourselves out and end up dying empty?

Deeply immersed in such thoughts, I asked myself: Why am I here? What is the purpose of my life? It is an exciting question. The answers are even more exciting. I invite you to try the following.

Exercise:

Set a stopwatch to 60 seconds and answer the question "Why am I here?" and then write down the answer. Re-set the clock and ask yourself, "Why am I here?" 60 seconds for the written answer... Repeat this a total of ten times and take exactly one minute for each answer.

After ten minutes, do you have ten answers to the same question right in front of you? Great! You are slowly getting to know yourself. Compare the answer to the first question with the last three answers on your sheet. How do they differ?

This little exercise is to show you how easy it is, with a little time and tenacity, to dig deeper and perhaps even come up with something amazing.

The Key to Yourself – Your Values

Working out your values is the next big step towards your free and successful life. Values are what we generally call the pillars of a personality. The pillars that support the pier above the water's surface – whether the water is calm or turbulent. The north star we use for orientation in our lives.

A series of factors, including background, childhood, spiritual beliefs, experiences, and one's own life philosophy, play a role here and yield a picture of your value system. The best days of our lives are those lived according to our values. Do you know your values? Which ones do you live by fully and which ones are you falling short on?

Exercise:

Find your values.

1. Selection
   Select ten of the values below from the value box. Don't think too much about it. Follow your gut feeling.

2. Reduction I
   Now cross out five of the values.

3. Reduction II
   Cross out two more of the remaining five values.

4. Prioritization
   Now arrange the three remaining values in a sequence of 1–3.

5. Examination
   Slowly read your top three values so that you understand and feel what those values mean to you and your life.

6. **Measuring**
   How much do you currently live up to the respective values? On a scale from -10 (not at all) to +10 (fully and completely), write a number in the respective box.

7. **Living up to the values**
   Now write the degree to which you would like to live up to these values (up to +10) and by when. Write in the box with the minus what has prevented you so far from living up to them, and in the box with the plus what you want to do differently now in order to live up to the values.

FAMILY HAPPINESS ☐ Quality time, Closeness -10 0 +10 -_____ +_____	**SELF-RESPECT** ☐ Self-preservation, Identity -10 0 +10 -_____ +_____	**GENEROSITY** ☐ Social Engagement -10 0 +10 -_____ +_____
COMPETITION Achieving success, taking risks	**RECOGNITION** Acknowledgment, status	**WISDOM** Converting information into knowledge and experience
FRIENDSHIP Building and maintaining resilient relationships	**CAREER** Progress in one's profession	**SPIRITUALITY** Religious or spiritual development
CARE Love, affection	**HEALTH** Mentally, physically	**CLARITY** Inner certainty, consistency

COOPERATION Collaboration with others, teamwork	**RESPONSIBILITY** Standing up for one's actions, achieving goals	**TRADITION** Cultivating cultural characteristics
ADVENTURE New challenges	**FAME** Public recognition	**INNER HARMONY** To have congruence
VITALITY Physical fitness, sports, strength	**JOY** Fun, relaxation	**INTEGRITY** Straightforwardness, standing up for oneself
PROSPERITY Earning money, becoming rich	**FINANCIAL FREEDOM** Plannable income, retirement provision	**CREATIVITY** Innovative actions, reinventing oneself
PERFORMANCE Achieving goals	**BELONGING** Belonging to a group	**ORDER** Planning and stability
FREEDOM Independence, authenticity	**INFLUENCE** Authority, controlling others	**PERSONAL DEVELOPMENT** Tapping into one's personal potential

8. Price

   Take some time and realize what price must be paid to give up the old (destructive / seemingly safe) behaviour. Imagine what is possible if you become active instead and leave your comfort zone.

9. Strategy

    Visualize how you are when you live your new behaviour. How will others react? What effect does that have on you? What feelings does imagining this invoke? What do you see, hear or smell? How does it taste to be what you want to be? Write or paint a picture/metaphor of it and anchor it this way in your subconscious mind.

10. Measuring

    Plan fixed times in the mornings and in the evenings. Take a few minutes to reflect. Keep a diary and record the realization of your values daily on this scale. Observe the changes.

    Congratulations! You've taken the first step.

Guide for everyday life.

1. Ask yourself the following questions when disoriented: Who do I want to be? Which action corresponds to this image? Should the image show you doing sports, then do sports. If the image of you does NOT want to eat ice cream, do not eat any. Awareness provides strength and orientation.

2. It is never too late for a happy childhood. No matter what was kept away or taken away from you as a child, resources have sprung up within you that open the door to a fulfilled life today. Look for them. You already know the shortcomings.

3. Do not take yourself and life too seriously. Ask yourself if what is currently driving you will still be of importance to you a year from now. Everything is relative.

4. Put order in your life. Clean out your home, get your documents in order, and bring clarity and planning to your finances.

5. Not every battle must be fought. Rather than "being right", you can also simply "have a different opinion."

6. Accept your life and your past. Even if not everything went as you had imagined. Self-condemnation only stands in the way of self-acceptance.

7. Comparison always kills happiness. You can only live your own life. Energy follows your focus. So why waste energy?

8. A painter paints, a gardener grows flowers. What is it that you enjoy? Just do it!

9. Don't suppress your feelings. If you are sad, be sad. Cry if you feel like it. Let it go. There is no award for self-pity.

10. Why wait? Nothing of what we expect is certain. Wear what you want to wear, do what you want to do. Days turn into special days when you make them so, not by waiting for them.

11. Consistent practice and good preparation. The archer practices every day. He thoroughly prepares for his training and the moment he has his target in sight, he connects with it and shoots his arrows while being at one with himself. We call this being "in the flow" or "in the zone".

12. Make the most of your opportunities. He who wants to win the lottery should at least buy a lottery ticket. The more tickets you buy, the higher the chance of winning. Whatever you wish for in life, increase the stakes, then switch into archer mode.

Happiness is our natural state. Moments of happiness are our golden moments.

What are your precious moments in life? Those small moments when you felt great, invincible and strong? Moments when everything was just right. They make life worth living. Moments in which we feel complete...

- Dancing and enjoying the music, no matter how it looks.
- Running in the rain without an umbrella and enjoying every single drop.
- Knowing one has closed the deal after a meeting.

- The feeling of being in love and having that feeling reciprocated.
- Laughing heartily and infecting others with one's cheerfulness.
- Getting up for the first time after an illness and feeling that one is healthy.
- The fragrance of sunshine after a long winter.
- _____
- _____
- _____
- _____
- _____

Take the time to enjoy these moments and celebrate your successes. Life keeps them ready for each of us at any time. Be ready, too.

Tip:

Take a few minutes every evening to write in your diary and jot down the small or big moments of gratitude, joy and confidence, so it may become a treasure chest for your golden moments. Your very own treasure chest: filled by you.

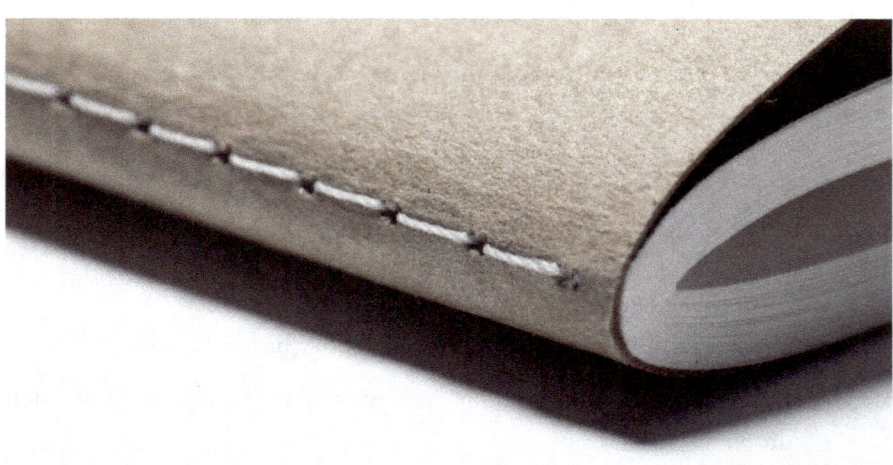

CHAPTER II

Decision

"Maybe" never gets hot.
"Lukewarm" is a decision too.

- Regina Reitinger -

Your life is the sum of your decisions. Good decisions thus make for a good life. What is your definition of a good decision?

_____

_____

_____

_____

In the course of evolution, our organism has learned to use its resources as efficiently as possible. Routines promise efficiency. As the main organ of the central nervous system, the brain is interested in working as efficiently as possible and conserving resources. We, therefore, run in autopilot mode throughout 90% of the days of our everyday life. Our consciousness surfs through habits and thought patterns of yesterday and automatically retrieves stored and readily available information. Otherwise we would have to learn every day anew whether and how to drink our coffee, where to find our way to work, or how the ticket machine works. This is clever and makes total sense because only in this way can we actually survive in everyday life.

However, when it comes to change, that autopilot will be of no help. We must actively take over the helm and leave everyday consciousness behind. On the so-called meta-level, i.e. the vantage point from which we can overlook our life from a higher perspective, we create the necessary distance. This book wants to help you to gain a first overview, to recognize connections, and to discover dependencies. Working with a coach or therapist can subsequently be helpful.

In the reflective consciousness, we recognize the patterns of our inner attitude and the resulting actions and decisions. It is said that there are two main motivators for our decisions. Love and fear.

The basic sources of our actions either feed on fear (loss/insecurity) or love (courage/trust). Understanding which source decides one's own actions is crucial. Do we act out of the inner state of "fear of ..." or "love of ..."?

What does that mean in our everyday life? What does this mean in situations where we ask ourselves the questions: "Go or stay?" "Do it or leave it?"

Lists of advantages and disadvantages may appear helpful for the sake of a first overview, but we should be aware that such advantages and disadvantages arise from the (unconsciously) prevailing inner state. What's in it for me to leave my comfort zone?

Fear will always find disadvantages in order to ride something out, to do something, or to finish something prematurely. Oddly enough, the fear of an abrupt end is usually smaller than the fear of showing oneself. To rethink something or stand up to one's viewpoint.

Those who want to go and yet remain silent never learn to use their wings, and end up watching others fly instead. Those who go away without trying to do something different may walk faster, but won't fly either.

Directions for qualitative decision-making:

1. *Building block: Clarity*

Start on the outside.

Which external factors affect your situation from your point of view and make a decision necessary?

Who could be affected by your decision?

Who would object to it? Who would be for it?

What effect would your decision have on your private life, on your job, on friends and your financial situation?

Grab a pad of sticky notes and write each point on a separate note. Stick these notes to the wall, or a large piece of paper. Let them sink in.

Now turn your attention inside.

What effects will the decision have on you and your understanding of yourself and on life in general?

What is its impact on your life?

Would you like more or less of these consequences in the future?

What do you gain, what do you lose?

What learning experience do you get from it?

What will improve in the future? What are you going to do for it, starting right now?

This approach will provide an overview and clarity on the current topic. Clarity is the first building block for qualitative decisions.

2. *Building block: Fear*

Short-circuit reactions and decisions based thereon usually follow from the unconscious attitude of fear. We look through the glasses of fear and experience and evaluate the situations and people accordingly. In doing so, we disregard our own behaviour that led us to influence the situations according to our pattern. Evaluation without self-reflection only leads to a collection of events without any learning experience. These "collected events" confirm what one had already assumed (glasses), while also keeping one in the helpless role of the victim. The currently experienced situation, however, does not change, but instead one continuously replenishes the negative account connected with the situation, partner or friend. This goes on until it feels like too much. Relief is urgently needed. Ideally immediately and forcefully. What follows are short-circuit reactions that usually manifest themselves in abrupt withdrawals, accusations, reproaches and breakups.

Decisions induced this way reflect the unconscious fear and that fear has many faces. Fear of injury, appropriation, vulnerability, intimacy, loss of control, of losing oneself. Our strategies for evading it are at least as varied. And since we would rather not face it out of a fear of fear, it maintains a firm grip on us. Our actions and thus our lives are determined by fear.

This is like being afraid of water and running a course that has a water jump 100m from the finish. The goal thus becomes unattainable. Even if one takes a detour to avoid the ditch. Fear of water has rendered the goal unreachable, or only reachable after long detours.

Invite the fear.

The strategy of learning to swim and thereby overcoming the fear of water seems more efficient and useful than continuing to shy away from it. *To do so, it is necessary to understand that fear.*

Take a look at your diagram from building block 1 and write down the fears in it for each topic. Stick the notes onto them which say: "I fear ..." You will find that it is not easy to clearly state the fear that lies in a topic. But naming the fear alone already leads to the first approaching.

The next step is to look the fear in the eye and ask it where it comes from and what it wants to tell you. What is its purpose?

Exercise:

- Take a larger sheet of paper, write the fear on it in large letters and place it on the floor.
- Stand about 3–5 metres away and look at the sheet on the floor.
- Which picture, which figure, which colour symbolizes this fear?
- How great is it from 0 (very small) to enormous (10)?
- Slowly approach the sheet of paper, feel the closeness and intensity of the fear until you stand directly in front of it.

- Now slowly and deliberately walk through the fear by stepping over the paper and stopping behind it.
- Pause for a moment.
- What do you perceive? What do you hear, taste or smell? How does it feel in the stomach/chest?
- Write these feelings down and when it feels right to you, turn around and deliberately take the same route back to your starting position.
- How do you perceive the fear now?
- How big or small does it seem to you now on a scale of 0–10?
- Write down these values as well.
- Repeat these steps with every fear you have written down.

How have the fear values changed?

The fear can no longer exert an invisible influence because you have passed through it. You have perceived it – and you have survived! You are still alive, and the fear has lost much of its scare. How do you feel now?

Write down your inner state by completing the following sentences:

I am _____.

The others are _____.

Life is _____.

Now go through the questions from building block 1 again.

Is there a change?

What would you like to change or add?

What action results from this, here and now?

Congratulations!

Within a very short time, you have gained clarity and an overview of your current topic and, incidentally, confronted your fears.

CHAPTER III

Need vs. Selfishness

> Everything we
> do for ourselves,
> we also do for others,
> and everything we
> do for others,
> we also do for others.
>
> *- THICH NHAT HANH -*

Evaluations usually arise unconsciously from our inner attitude towards ourselves and life. We generally do not distinguish whether a person simply puts their own needs above those of another person – I will discuss this later – or whether they direct their actions only towards their own advantage and tacitly accepts the fact that another person suffers a disadvantage or damage as a result. But what is the meaning of the term selfishness or egotism as far as its origin is concerned?

Ego (Latin "I") -ism (Greek suffix) describes the ego-"centredness".

What does it mean to be self-centred?

Understood in the best sense of the word, the focus is on oneself and one's own needs. The action is thus oriented towards the needs. Seen in this light, there is nothing wrong with it as long as you don't take anything away from others that does not belong to you. On the contrary, looking after one's own well-being is, in my view, the most fundamental responsibility we have in life. Who else, if not ourselves, should spend a lifetime looking after our physical, mental and emotional well-being?

Unconscious egotism is based on one's personal benefit, not on one's own needs. Those who are aware of their needs and act accordingly will act in a clear and authentic manner. However, the degree of one's own state of consciousness plays a key role. See Chapter 1. Those who act unconsciously and without reflection are as unfamiliar with their own needs as those who adapt their own behaviour according to others in the hope of being recognized and loved. While the one acts out of greed, the other acts out of dependency.

Those who pay attention to their well-being, be it physical or mental health, act in a positive sense of self-love. Self-love means knowing oneself and knowing what one needs and what one does not. Anyone who acts in a clear and consistent manner and does not take anything away from others is aware of their own self and thus of their own needs.

How do you recognize this dependency? We often confuse our own needs with our expectations. Expectations of others we believe we must meet. Childhood conditioning may be responsible for whether and how we feel obliged to meet unspoken or assumed expectations. The underlying needs may be, for example needs such as recognition, appreciation, love, harmony, etc. The resulting behaviour is thus completely controlled from the outside and has nothing to do with our own needs.

In this context, I would like to tell you the story of Paula. Paula is 48 years old and someone one would generally be referred to as a family person. Paula grew up as the youngest of three siblings. Her two brothers were nine and seven years older than she was. The last thing the two had in mind was taking care of their younger sister. But Paula wanted to belong. But neither in arguments nor in fights did she have a chance to assert herself against her brothers, so she had to develop and resort to a different strategy to finally be seen and to belong. She quickly learned that she could score with her brothers when she took over their household chores or prepared their lunch sandwiches.

She grew up. It had long since become normal for her to take over the unpleasant tasks for her brothers, to cover up for them with white lies to their parents and always sympathetically listening to their problems. In exchange, they occasionally took her with them to a party or introduced her to their friends. So her strategy worked. She took over tasks for others and thus belonged to the group.

The years passed. Paula was now 48 years old, had since married one of her brothers' friends early on and had two children who were already studying and no longer living at home. Her life went on unchanged following the same patterns. One such tradition was that the whole family would come together for coffee and home-baked cake every Sunday afternoon. It was an unwritten law that the family met at her place on Sundays. That Sunday coffee meeting would even take place when she was sick or unwell. She had never questioned it. She had never asked herself if she actually wanted that.

One day, when she was coming back from her morning run, she saw her neighbour leaving the house carrying suitcases. She greeted her and cheerfully shouted that she just needed a little holiday now and would be back in three weeks.

Paula stopped and waited until the neighbour had stepped into a taxi, and as she stood there and waved after her, she wondered what it would be like if she did the same thing. She had never gone on vacation alone. She had not even left home for a weekend. And, after all, how would she have done so? What would her husband and the rest of the family have thought? After all, she was the one who kept everything together. There was no way she could just drive away.

"Can I not?" She could suddenly hear a previously unknown voice in her head. "Can I really not?" The question became even louder, so that she did not hear her husband's voice until he was standing right behind her. She was still looking in the direction where her neighbour's taxi had long since disappeared, her hand still raised in greeting. As if in a trance, she followed her husband into the house.

The noise of the shower blended with the resounding voice in her head. What was wrong with her? It was Friday morning and time to get ready for the day, but somehow it was as though someone had built an oversized brake in her head and her body.

She had trouble completing her daily to-do lists. Again and again, she saw the taxi drive off with her neighbour. The voice in her head became more demanding: "What is stopping you? What are you waiting for?"

She was sitting at her kitchen table with the coffee cup in her hand seeing her childhood and her whole life before her. Had she not always been the kind one, the one who took care of things and the one you could always count on? But wasn't it also true that she owed everything to her brothers? Where would she be without them? Yes, where would she be? She had never really asked that question. She wanted to be liked. She wanted to participate. She had never actually thought of her own needs. And, after all, how would she have done so? She had not learned that up to now.

She pictured what it would be like if she just packed her bags and went off on vacation for a few weeks. She was overcome by a sudden lightness she had never experienced before. At the same time, she was also excited, her heart beating wildly. Her travelling alone without her family? ALONE? At the same time, an insane fear overcame her that almost took her breath away.

What would her brothers, her husband and her children say about that? How would they react?

False altruism is just as destructive as reckless egotism. Both are based on fear. While fear of not getting recognized or integrated (> lack of self-love) prevails in dependency, ruthless egotism arises out of fear of the desired resource being insufficiently available (> lack of confidence).

Paula could no longer find her way back into her usual everyday life. She was exhausted and came to my office one day. She told me her story, and in the course of our work together she not only realized that she had only been living the value of belonging in external relationships, but also that she had developed a strong dependence on the people around her while having built up no relationship with herself and her needs. She became painfully aware of her massive lack of self-love and how she had deluded herself throughout her whole life.

Over the course of our systemic process work, she gradually dissolved old belief patterns. From the observer position, she was able to recognize and re-programme her very own programme. Her way of thinking about herself fundamentally changed. Things which had hitherto seemed impossible suddenly appeared normal to her.

The Sunday meetings are long gone. She has bought herself a racing bicycle and is training for an international bicycle race. The rejection she had feared never occurred. On the contrary, after some initial confusion, her family has been actively supporting her so that she can easily integrate regular training trips into her day. She has learned to sense and communicate her needs.

CHAPTER IV

Clarity and Action

There is only one success:
to be able to spend life
in your own way.

- Christopher Morley -

Imagine you wake up one morning and all those voices of inner doubters, judges and prosecutors have fallen silent. No one left to tell you that you are not good enough or of too little worth. No one before whom you must have a bad conscience or whom you need to ask for permission.

At first you might think, oh, how great, then I'd finally have my peace and quiet. But then what? I'd like to tell you the story of Franco. Franco's life generally corresponded to what would be commonly referred to as well-off middle class. Good education, doctor in a large clinic, married, two children. Franco was the eldest of three children. His father was a doctor too, and he had learned early on to take responsibility for his younger siblings. Good grades at school went without saying. He sensed the expectations of his parents from an early age and became part of his understanding of how one had to be. It shaped his way of thinking, acting and judging and thus his individual value system (attitude).

The values anchored in the hidden part of the mountain become visible on the visible peak of behaviour. For Franco, these values were above all a sense of duty and reason. Based on this, it seemed natural to him to take the same profession as his father. He chose his wife according to the same principle. Paula, his wife, was a dear, reliable partner with whom he had two children. They lived in a beautiful house not far from his clinic.

The years passed. The children were already almost grown up and life proceeded in an orderly fashion, until that one morning. Franco had a very intense dream. He awoke with the sound of the sea still in his ear. Slightly confused and yet with a clear view like never before. Instead of driving to the clinic as usual, he drove to the train station and boarded the train headed for the coast. It was only a two hour drive and yet he could not remember the last time he had driven out to the sea. Throughout the whole ride, he felt like he was flying over the landscape himself. He could literally smell the morning mist of the grass and feel the warmth of the sun on his skin. His head was empty. No thought of his clinic. He had not even checked out. No thought of Paula. Nothing. The train had reached its final destination. He got off the train slowly and crossed the small station square, heading directly for the coast. The warm wind in his hair, the sun on his skin. He breathed the salty air into his lungs like a drowning man gasping for air.

Later, when he felt his lungs and head were thoroughly cleansed, he sat on the terrace of a restaurant overlooking the waves. The sound of the waves put him into a more and more relaxed state. He enjoyed the moment.

Enjoying the moment. That was new.

He did not know the answer to the question: What am I actually doing here? Suddenly it was not important that no one knew where he was, and also that he was absent for the first time unexcused at work. He, the reasonable doctor and reliable family man, suddenly had no answer to his behavior.

Despite his outward clam, or because of it, his thoughts got going fast. He got himself paper and pen and started to write. His hand raced across the paper. At some point he leaned back, exhausted and tired. The writing on the pages before him scared him.

When he unlocked the front door a few hours later and stepped into the hallway of his familiar house, everything suddenly seemed so strange to him. The hoped-for feeling of familiarity and security did not set in. But instead a new clarity. He suddenly knew what had to be done.

What happened?

Because of his dream, Franco left his everyday life >> Jump from the top of the iceberg into the ice-cold water. He questioned his values and reflected on his previous actions >> expedition to the lower part of the iceberg. His previous life felt strange and he was at the beginning of his change >> dissolution and rearranging of old patterns and values hidden in the invisible part of the iceberg.

A change of perspective and the view from a new distance opens the door to a new view of oneself. Thus, relationships and repetitions due to inner programmes can be identified and resolved. Letting go of old beliefs creates space and thus clarity and consistency.

Change of action (consciously) through a real change of attitude (unconsciously) manifests itself in clear communication and action. Conscious orientation to one's own volition replaces the unconscious "supposed to do's" for others. Consistency and demarcation create respect and space for oneself. We cannot get anything from others that we haven't already given ourselves.

Freedom is the abandonment of self-made attachment and dependency and has nothing to do with the reckless and irresponsible flight behaviour it is often confused with. While the needy clings to a desired outcome and is devastated when it does not happen, the one who takes an inner decision for or against something remains unscathed no matter what the outcome looks like.

CHAPTER V

Focus and Goal

The fear of missing the target is in itself no reason to stop the shot.

- Paulo Coelho / The Way of the Bow -

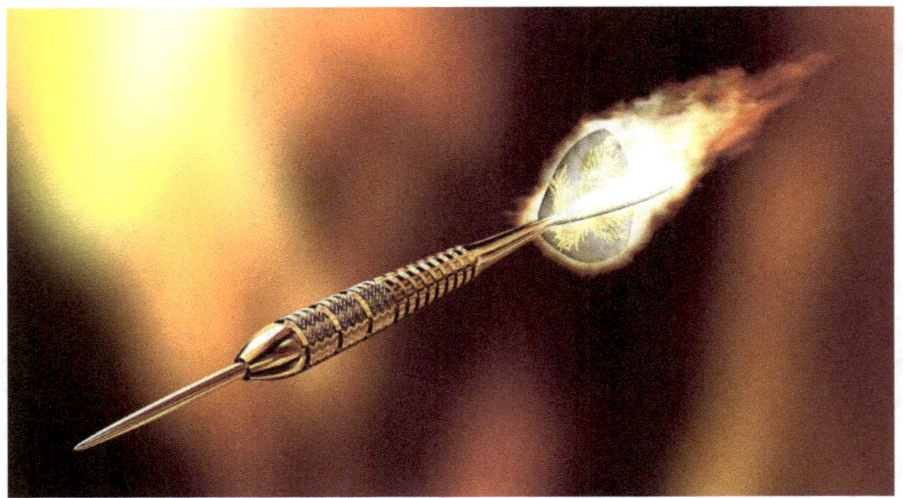

Everything in life has its price. He who wants to be loud will be heard and must expect that not everyone will like it. Those who withdraw into their comfort zone and remain silent pay the price of not being heard. The newfound clarity demands at the same time one's willingness and courage to pay its price. For change has its consequences and those also have to do with loss.

In the case of Franco, the losses were also manifold.

- Loss of his marriage due to different expectations
- This resulted in the loss of the previous family life
- Loss of the joint house
- Loss of his job

Does that mean that all those who give up their previous "should-life" and evolve into their "own-life" become the losers of society? No, on the contrary. You can recognize the "own-living persons" by the fact that they somehow move more freely in our society than others. Who do not HAVE to be for or against something, nor do they HAVE to position themselves. They are the so-called free spirits of our society. Those who swim against the current and ask uncomfortable questions. Who are guided by the present and the future rather than by the past. Flight is no longer necessary. It is completed.

Purpose and meaning form the prevailing basis for their actions. Neither time-honoured standards, nor so-called quick wins can impress them and will certainly not deter them from their overriding mission. Solo efforts that only encompass one's own benefit are uninteresting.

The demanding instinctive clarity will inevitably be felt, and even Franco could no longer escape it. After his inner cognition process, he was simply no longer able to live in false harmony. The dishonesty, cowardice and ambiguity inherent therein would have gone so far from his newly discovered self-image that it would simply have been impossible to continue the old life.

The new perspectives rendered the connecting points to Paula difficult and eventually impossible. As a result, the marriage broke apart. He left the house to her and the children and went to South America for a year to study among the indigenous peoples in the Amazon rainforest.

When he came back, he opened his own practice in which he applied the healing arts of the Brazilian indigenous peoples along with Western medicine. Within a very short time, he made his name as a naturopathy healer, gave lectures, and spent at least half of the year in the jungle. His life had changed completely, and his change was visible to everyone. He had become years younger. His cheerful and relaxed manner was contagious. People loved coming to him. He was successful and earned good money which he, unlike before, did not invest in a new home, but in his professional and personal development and in the support of projects that served society.

Once you have jumped into the cold water, you should continue to swim and then you will get warm again.

It might happen that you close the book now and say: Enough of this. This is all too much for me. If this is the solution, then I want my problem back!

Believe me, I can totally understand that. More than once, I stood at such a point in my life where I would have loved to just stick my head in the sand and continue as before. And each time it did not take long before something within me pulled me and dragged me and made me take the next step. And so, I went, and so I continue to go step by step through my inner development and my life. The valleys are not nearly as bleak as they used to be. And today I know that my courage and confidence will carry me through and beyond any doubts.

Take a look back and see what you wrote in chapter 1. How long will you be able to ignore the shortcomings in your life? Do you really want to continue giving in to your fear? Take the bow in your hand. Practice a little bit every day. One day, your desire to shoot will be greater than your fear. The source of charisma, personal radiance and the power of attraction is our inner serenity. The space we naturally occupy becomes brighter and wider.

CHAPTER VI

Agreements with Yourself

> Those who do what they intend can enjoy their success longer. Those who procrastinate their projects will always have a full agenda – but not success.
>
> *- Regina Reitinger -*

Studies prove that procrastination is an absolute mood killer. Are you one of those people who like a structured approach and, therefore, write down tasks on a To Do list? After that, are you busy transferring the list from one day to the next each day, without even completing a single item of it? Adding more and more tasks to the list instead, which in turn causes you more and more frustration? Do you share your frustration with the whole world by telling everyone how stressed you are and how you are not really getting anything done?

Time for reorganization.

While you continue to write down the tasks in an unstructured way,

- without weighting and
- without time details,

everything might be written down somewhere, but none of it gets done. Instead, the pressure and dissatisfaction concerning the "mountain" of undone tasks is steadily mounting.

Our brain does not like big **mountains.** Big mountains are like insurmountable obstacles. And because they are insurmountable, it finds strategies to somehow keep busy in order to not have to look at that mountain.

Our brain prefers to **play.**

> **Structure**
> **Prioritize**
> **Initiative**
> **Complete**
> **Let go**
> **Success**
> **Sustainability**

Structure

your tasks according to the WHY and divide them into areas such as job, household, children, travel, authorities, etc.

Prioritize

them according to importance, urgency and time required. Plan it in a way that it is definitely and realistically feasible for you.

Initiative

is what's called for. Get going on what you had planned for today. Prepare everything you need (e.g. documents, etc.) the night before. Today, the task you planned has priority 0 (= highest importance).

Complete

the tasks and complete what you set out to do.

Let go

of topics that don't belong. Delegate tasks to others, or if the WHY has no (longer) relevance to you, delete the point from the list.

Success

is what happens after that. Every checkmark you can put next to a completed task is your success. Each success, as small as it may be, encourages you to tackle the bigger issues in your life.

Sustainability

results from kept agreements. You simply dare to do more once you prove to yourself that you can rely on yourself.

Try it out and you'll see how much fun it can be to approach your tasks in a playful manner. And the delineation of the necessary time windows should no longer be a problem thanks to your newly won clarity. 😊

CHAPTER VII

Your Life – Good or Bad?

In the process of letting go you will lose a lot of things from the past but you will find yourself.

- Deepak Chopra -

When you trust yourself, you are more likely to take responsibility for your actions. In the previous chapters we looked at what it means to design a life full of self-connectedness. A life without adherence and adjustment. By now we know that all of this is not easy to attain, nor does it come cheap. Everything has its price.

Take a look at yourself, or, if you have started writing your journal by now, check your notes. How would you describe yourself? As a victim of circumstances or other people, or as a co-responsible person?

Aside from the fact that the way we see ourselves determines the inner freedom we feel, it is absolutely crucial to our inner satisfaction. Because it makes a difference whether we understand our lives as an interlinked field of energy and experience that is centered around ourselves, or whether we see it as a chain of circumstances, mistakes, and missed opportunities that have "happened" to us.

The statement "something has happened to me" carries a passive attitude within itself. It is therefore not my fault. Let's look at the example of Petra in this respect.

Petra was an open-minded young woman. Mid-40s, single mother of a 13-year-old son. She came to my practice because she was dissatisfied with her job and could not end her relationship in which she was cheated on and lied to by her partner.

The initial interview revealed that neither the professional situation nor the nature of the relationship was new to her. She knew both from different past experiences in her life. She was the unlucky person. She simply had no luck. Neither with her job selection nor with men.

A fixed negative attribution had her pick that one option from among the stream of possibilities flowing past her which was liable to reconfirm and reinforce that negative attribution over and over again. The experiences repeated themselves. The vicious circle was perfect. Her way of thinking about herself and her real-life experiences confirmed each other.

However, she was not aware of the dynamics of this system until then. In the course of the system clarification in the further sessions, she learned to see herself as part of her system (life/world/cosmos) and to experience herself as part of the whole. That was unusual for Petra at first. Throughout all those years, the virus infection had stealthily formed her personality and shaped her individual experience to such an extent that it was perfectly normal and logical to her to unquestionably identify herself with it as a person. The following self-statement clearly expresses this:

"I am Petra the unlucky one. My boss ignores me, my colleagues bully me. My partner is lying to and cheating on me. The world is unfair and dishonest."

Everything is already present in every cell of our body. Total universal knowledge is stored there in comprehensive completeness and it is in constant communication with all life in this universe. However, an overwriting of this universal master programme by a virus has taken place. Forgetting and a feeling of imperfection is characteristic of this virus. This virus is activated at birth and continues to spread throughout childhood, in the course of which we are raised and educated by those who are also infected – all the way into adulthood. The state in which we feel inferior, unloved or disconnected and weak has already evolved into a fixed part of our personality and manifested itself as such. See Petra's statement about herself above.

Identification has taken full effect, and because of the fear of being discovered, a variety of strategies have been developed to prevent others from noticing it. These are, for example,

- Performance that is exhausting to the point of chronic overstrain.
- Excessive accumulation of knowledge in order not to be regarded as stupid, yet fear of putting that knowledge into action,
- Excessive adjustment for fear of rejection or withdrawal of love.
- Belittling oneself for weak partners because one does not feel attractive and competent enough for a loving and appreciative partnership.

Sentences expressing these strategies are, for example:

- That's not for me, others can do it better.
- When someone gets to know me better, he or she will see that I'm not that great after all.
- I always have to outperform others, so they don't notice that I'm actually a pretender and do not actually deserve the job / money / reputation, etc.
- You can't have everything in life. You just have to make compromises sometimes.
- I have to be satisfied with what I have.
- If I want to have more, I have to take something away from someone else.
- I have to be smarter than others so as not to get cheated.

The own perception is absolutely marked by scarcity.

I'm not enough and helpless.

Others don't like me. I don't belong. I have to be on guard against people who want to cheat me.

Love, happiness and money are scarce commodities. I have to fight for it and/or work hard for it.

The paradox of it is that even though life is being experienced as difficult and unsatisfactory, nothing is being done to change the situation. Instead, the strategy is being further fine-tuned in order to somehow compensate for the whole thing. Dissatisfaction remains and happiness is something you must actively hunt down.

True liberation only sets in when one has managed to change the perspective. In other words, when one sees oneself as the one causing action rather than receiving it, and therefore uses the power that was always available with the original master programme.

Petra gradually dissolved the patterns created by the mis-programming and thus found her inner strength and self-confidence. She learned to love and value herself. The resulting self-respect simply did not allow any further humiliation.

She quit her job and found a new position where she could contribute her skills and develop further. She left her partner, and together with her son, she moved into a beautiful bright apartment with a garden which she found quickly and furnished cosily.

Two years later, she visited me in my practice and I barely recognized her. What had become of the low-spirited, restrained person of those days? Cheerful eyes glowed at me from a youthful-looking, fresh face. She confidently and energetically told me about the developments in her life. About her son, who was able to cope with everyday life in a quiet and focused manner without any ADHD medication, about the new leadership role she had taken on and about her happy partnership which makes her feel loved and supported. The inner transformation could not be overlooked. She had arrived at the centre of her energy field and deliberately steered the fortunes of her life with it.

To be in the centre of one's own energy field does not mean that one now floats on a pink cloud, but rather that one accepts the circumstances and learns to actively deal with them. What is, is. No more energy is wasted on if's and but's or would's, supposed to's and should have's.

Phrases like, "If I were younger / older, male / female, taller / smaller, bigger / thinner etc., then ...", "He / she would just have to ... then ...", "In another city / apartment it would be much better, but as things stand ..." are no longer valid.

The key to happiness is accepting what is. Those who cause action, the act-ors, find ways to change things. Those who are subjected to action, the act-ees, find reasons why something cannot happen. Who are you?

CHAPTER VIII

Mistakes – Opportunities for Experiences

> Be brave. Take risks. Nothing can substitute experience.
>
> *- Paulo Coelho –*

In the example of Petra, we have seen that it is possible to resolve self-damaging mis-programming and to give life a new direction by accessing the underlying master programme. This is, in fact, not only possible, but necessary. Because anyone who thinks in error mode will do nothing but evaluate: themselves and others. With those in evaluation mode, the virus is fully effective. One's own actions are judged as good or bad. But according to what standards? And above all, the evaluators must assume that they, too, are being evaluated. This closes the circle of evaluation, assumed expectations and the avoidance strategies used to avoid negative evaluation by others.

A rather tight corset, don't you think? Anyone not wanting to end up in the notorious cycle of energy waste on endless strategy streamlining needs another way. But what is the antidote to widespread and universally recognized evaluation?

The formula for breaking this cycle may seem a bit old-fashioned at first. Being unspectacular and a little out of fashion, it may even sound somewhat religiously inspired to some people. To some, the current buzz word "mindfulness" may fit better. What I'm talking about are the simple fundamental characteristics of human existence: Gratitude, humility, mercy, and forgiveness.

1. Forgive yourself for not being perfect. Perfectionism is not a state to be desired. If it takes too long, you'll be dead first.

2. Show mercy. Others don't exist to annoy you, nor to make you happy. You determine your own reaction to others.

3. Respect the power within yourself. Use it carefully to design your life in a self-effective manner.

4. Be grateful for every day you can open your eyes and find yourself healthy and alive. Appreciate the small things. Taken together, they bring about great things.

I invite you to take on the challenge of resisting evaluation each day anew. Start with yourself and become the queen/king of your kingdom.

- Allow yourself to be the best version of yourself and learn in the course of it.

- Ask yourself what is good for you and whether you can and want to bear the consequences of your decision.

- Make a pact with yourself that you will not blame yourself or see yourself as a victim, regardless of the outcome. Write it down.

- Make your own decisions regardless of what others might say.

- Despite the pressure of high waters on all sides, you will pass through every storm unscathed with your dignity and your head held high.

- Even when you seem to be at a dead end. There is always still another trump card: HUMOUR. 😊

CHAPTER IX

Be Good to Yourself

Peace is the result of retraining your mind to process life as it is, rather than as you think it should be.

- Wayne Dyer -

Imagine lying in bed with your eyes closed, while your senses are aware of all the noise around you and you carry these with you into the demimonde between sleep and wakefulness. This makes for wild mixtures of reality and dreams as you blissfully and weightlessly float through dream worlds ... until a loud honking jolts you suddenly and without warning out of your sleep and brings you back to reality. No more floating.

Reality.

We have learned to evaluate that which we see in our waking state through our eyes as real, and all else as fiction. The truth, however, is that our brain does not distinguish whether we perceive and experience something through our eyes or only in our imagination. The brain does exactly the same in both cases. It issues orders to the hormone system to secrete the corresponding neurotransmitters.

Suppose you had an argument with your boss yesterday. You felt you were treated unfairly and got very upset about it. The argument went on for about ten minutes. If a sample of your blood would have been taken shortly afterwards, the laboratory examination would certainly have shown an increased value of the stress hormone Cortisol.

A day went by. The dispute is long over, but you keep thinking of it and you notice how the anger comes up again each time you replay the scene in your mind. If one were to take your blood sample again now, the lab report would be quite similar to yesterday's. Isn't that crazy? In addition to permanently poisoning our hours and days because of a ten minute incident, we also end up poisoning our bodies.

> "No one has ever died from a snake bite. They die from the venom which continues to pour through the system long after the bite took place."
>
> - Wayne Dyer

If this is the case and we can in fact trigger reactions in the body with our thoughts, would it not make perfect sense to use this power the other way around? How about imagining the best version of you each day anew? A mental image where you see and perceive yourself in all facets, looks, actions and feelings? The brain does its job and passes on the relevant information so that what is desired is not only thought, but also felt. The reprogramming of the body cells now starts. This is key for the new positive self-image based on which actions are initiated and reality is created.

Because these processes run subconsciously and can only be recognized through reflection, it takes that moment of becoming aware. Just like right now as you read these lines.

Now, you have the option of encoding your own body through your thinking and thereby create new realities.

The will to conceive oneself as one's best version has nothing to do with illusory arrogance. Instead, one ought to ask oneself how long history is to repeat itself due to the human species constantly operating below its potential and barring its own way to its innate resources. Change takes place where awareness grows, where new thinking occurs, and new actions are taken.

CHAPTER
X

The Best Version of You

You recognize yourself in others. Do you like what you see?

- Regina Reitinger -

Do you know someone who finds you irresistible and amazing? Do you know someone who wants to be with you? Someone who considers you the most perfect creature on earth?

When I started to write this book, I wished for _____ [YOUR NAME] to be written here.

I also wanted your journey log to reflect your personal success story on your journey to inner freedom. Simply for the reason that there are too many opportunities in our world one can get attached and tied to and thus end up stuck in the material world. Those who focus their actions on the attainment of material possessions or security will never achieve inner freedom since their security is tied to something outside of them. If security can only be achieved through a sum of x euros in one's bank account, what happens if this sum of x euros is not or no longer there?

How free is one really if all one's actions are solely aimed at achieving this sum of x euros? Who am in relation to all of this? The creator or slave of that sum? Isn't stable inner freedom only within reach of those who act from a deep conviction and conscious being? Doesn't it logically follow that the sum of x euros then flows into one's account as if by itself, as a result of one's actions?

Your personal travel report:

1. My self-image: _____
   _____

2. The source of my decisions is _____
   _____

3. Recognizing and identifying my needs means _____
   _____

4. My actions follow _____ and as a result
   _____

5. By acting in a focused and aware manner, my effect on others is _____
   _____

6. I implement my plans, as a result _____
   _____

7. To accept what is, allows me to _____
   _____

8. My experiences help me to _____
   _____

9. For me, pain is ——————————————————. Suffering is part of
   ————————————————————————————————

10. I describe myself as ——————————————————————
    ————————————————————————————————

Maybe you would like to send me a photo of your travel report? I would love to see it. Whatever you saw and experienced on your journey, it is your personal path that may have initially started with this book for you and thus served as your first stage companion, or it may have accompanied you on part of a journey you already started a while back.

Yours
Regina Reitinger

www.ingramcontent.com/pod-product-compliance
Lightning Source LLC
LaVergne TN
LVHW021950060526
838200LV00043B/1964